Transferring Energy

Torrey Maloof

Consultant

Michelle Alfonsi
Engineer, Southern California
Aerospace Industry

Publishing Credits

Rachelle Cracchiolo, M.S.Ed., *Publisher*
Conni Medina, M.A.Ed., *Managing Editor*
Diana Kenney, M.A.Ed., NBCT, *Senior Editor*
Dona Herweck Rice, *Series Developer*
Robin Erickson, *Multimedia Designer*
Timothy Bradley, *Illustrator*

Image Credits: Cover, p.1 tzara/iStock; p.14 David
Nicholls / Science Source; p.21 Gary S. Settles / Science
Source; p.8 Iain Masterton / Alamy; pp.4, 6, 7, 9, 10, 12, 13,
16, 17, 20, 26 iStock; p.11 Jacopin / BSIP / Alamy; pp.28,
29 Janelle Bell-Martin; p.32 Martin Shields / Alamy; pp.13,
19 NASA; p.23 Science Source; pp.6, 7 Timothy J. Bradley;
all other images from Shutterstock.

Library of Congress Cataloging-In-Publication Data

Maloof, Torrey, author.
  Transferring energy / Torrey Maloof.
    pages cm
  Includes index.
  ISBN 978-1-4807-4683-1 (pbk.)
1. Energy transfer--Juvenile literature. 2. Force and
energy--Juvenile literature. I. Title.
  QC73.8.E53M35 2016
  531.6--dc23
                        2014045206

Teacher Created Materials

5301 Oceanus Drive
Huntington Beach, CA 92649-1030
http://www.tcmpub.com

ISBN 978-1-4807-4683-1

Table of Contents

Energy Is Everywhere

It's a chilly winter morning. The heater in your home kicks on just as your alarm clock begins to sound. With your eyes still closed, you fumble in the dark, feeling along the wall for the light switch. Flip! With one easy motion, your room is flooded with light. You silence your alarm, take a deep breath, and slowly open your eyes. You're ready to start your day. The heater in your home, the alarm clock by your bed, and the lights in your room all run on **energy**. You run on energy, too! Energy is everywhere!

You use energy to get out of bed, get dressed, and brush your teeth. Energy powers the bike you ride to school, keeps airplanes in the sky, and runs the cars that drive past you on the road. Everywhere you look, energy is at work. But what exactly is energy?

Caveman Style

The oldest source of energy that humans use is fire. We didn't begin using other sources, such as wind, until about 5,000 years ago. The first power plant wasn't even built until 1882.

4

Energy powers a dirt bike.

The average American family spends about $2,000 a year on energy bills.

Energy at Work

Energy is the power or ability to do some type of **work**. When scientists use the word *work*, they mean "movement." They are referring to the motion of atoms, molecules, and larger objects. In other words, energy sets things in motion!

Pretend you're rowing a boat on a lake. You push the oars forward. Then, you pull the oars back. This pushing and pulling propels, or moves, the boat. You're using force to move something. You're using energy to do work!

The push and pull of oars on the water results in work, which is the boat moving!

There are two types of energy: stored and active. Active energy is known as **kinetic energy**. It's the energy of motion. It's working energy. Stored energy is called **potential energy**. It's energy that can be used later. Now, imagine a book sitting on a table. The book has potential energy. If you use your hand to push the book off the table, you're using kinetic energy. When the book falls, its potential energy changes to kinetic energy.

{ If you double the speed of an object, its kinetic energy increases by four times. }

Powerful Potential

The heavier an object is and the higher off the ground it is, the more potential energy it has. *Harry Potter and the Order of the Phoenix* is over 800 pages! That book sitting on a high table sure has a lot of potential energy!

A great example of kinetic and potential energy is a roller coaster. Machines in the track pull the car up to the top of the first hill. The machines' energy is stored in the car as potential energy. The car climbs higher and higher. It gains more potential energy. When it reaches the top of the hill, it has a lot of potential energy. The machines stop pulling the car. The car begins to roll down the hill. All that potential energy is finally released as the car zooms down the track. The potential energy has turned into kinetic energy. Riders scream as the car picks up speed. You won't hear the machines working anymore because the car is gliding on its own. Next time you ride a roller coaster, pay attention to the way the car moves before and after a drop.

Formula Rossa is the world's fastest roller coaster with speeds that reach 240 kilometers per hour (149 miles per hour)!

Transferring Energy

Did you know that energy can't be created or destroyed? Instead, it just changes forms or transfers from one object to another. It's indestructible! Let's look at the different ways energy moves.

Remember that book we pushed off a table? What happened when the book hit the floor? Its potential energy turned into kinetic energy as the book fell. Then, it hit the ground and sent vibrations through the air. Energy was released in the form of sound. Thud!

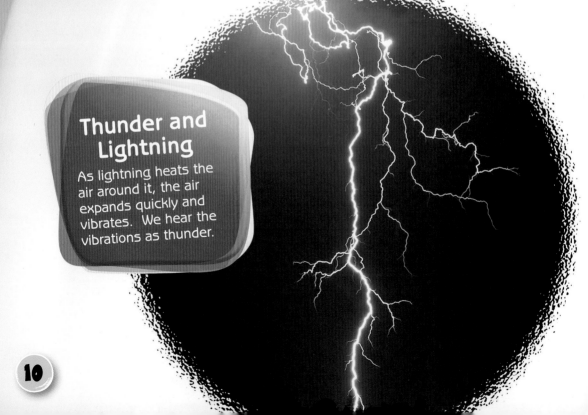

Thunder and Lightning

As lightning heats the air around it, the air expands quickly and vibrates. We hear the vibrations as thunder.

BANG! CRASH! BOOM!

Sound in Motion

Bang! Crash! Boom! Sound is a wave of energy created by vibrations moving through matter. The vibrations move the air around and create a **sound wave**. The sound wave travels to your ear and moves down your ear canal. Then, the sound wave bounces into your eardrum. Next, your eardrum sends a message to your brain and your brain tells you what the sound is.

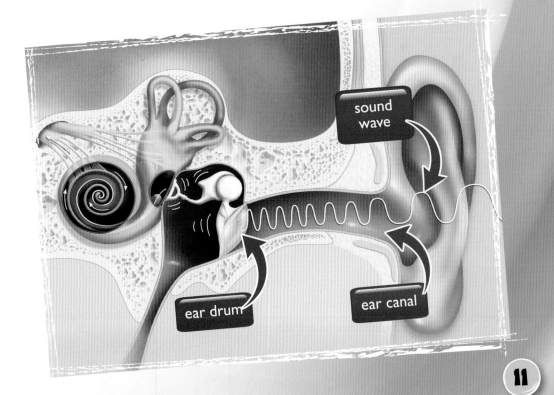

sound wave

ear drum

ear canal

Sound waves carry energy. When energy hits a surface, such as a wall, it bounces back creating an echo or a copy of the sound. There are many different kinds of sounds. If you blow a whistle, you create a high-pitched sound. High-pitched sounds have a high number of sound waves per second. The sound waves move quickly. If you bang a drum, you create a low-pitched sound. This means there are fewer sound waves per second and they move more slowly.

Compression Wave

When an object creates a sound wave, the air molecules compress together, and then expand. The distance between one compression and the next is the wavelength of the sound wave.

Have you ever seen a singer break a glass using his or her voice? Maybe you saw it on television or in a cartoon. Well, this can really happen! The singer sings a high-pitched note. Energy is transferred from the sound of the note to the air. The vibrations travel to the glass. The vibrations become so strong that eventually the glass shatters and breaks!

Sound travels faster through water than it does through air.

Can You Hear Me Now?

If you need some peace and quiet, you should travel to outer space. Sound needs matter to travel. Because there is no matter in outer space, there is also no sound.

Light in Motion

Did you know that life on Earth wouldn't exist without the sun? The light from the sun supplies Earth with energy. Plants, animals, and humans all need light energy to survive.

Light from the sun radiates, or travels, in waves through space. Sunlight travels about 150 million kilometers (93 million miles) to get to Earth. When you look at the night sky, you see stars that are much farther away than the sun. The stars are so far away that the distance is measured in light years. A light year is the distance that light travels in one year. The sun is too close for its distance to be measured in light years. The sun's light gets to Earth in 8 minutes and 20 seconds.

Transforming Light

Light is transformed into another type of energy when it reaches Earth. Plants use a process called *photosynthesis* to change light energy into **chemical energy**.

In one minute, the sun provides Earth with enough energy to last a year.

Radiant Energy

Radiant energy is another term for light energy. Radiant energy includes visible light, X-rays, gamma rays, and radio waves.

You may be wondering how the sun gives us energy. Let's take a look. The sun shines its light energy down on Earth. Plants use this energy to live and grow. Plants also store some of it as chemical energy. When we eat plants, the stored energy is transferred into our bodies. Then we can use that energy to do work! The same is true with animals. Animals eat plants and transfer the energy into their bodies. Then, when a human eats an animal, the energy is transferred again. The energy is never destroyed. Rather, it is passed along from one living thing to the next.

Innovative Technology

The Tesla Roadster has a regenerative braking system. When you take your foot off the gas or press on the brake, the kinetic energy in the car is changed into chemical energy and is stored in the car's battery. Regenerative braking recharges the battery!

The Tesla Roadster can drive nearly 394 km (245 mi.) per charge!

Tesla Roadster

solar panels

Since the sun shows up every day, we can use its light energy in other ways! Did you know that sunlight can be turned into electricity? We do this by using solar cells. Solar cells can be grouped in large panels that sit in a sunny area. The cells in the panels transfer light energy into **electric energy**. That energy can run electric cars and heat homes.

Heat in Motion

Thermal energy is another form of energy. Think about the molecules and atoms inside an object. These are **particles**, and they are in motion. They move back and forth. The faster they move, the more energy they have. The more energy they have, the hotter they become. The energy the particles have is called *thermal energy*. Thermal energy is not the same as heat. Heat is the movement of thermal energy between two objects. There are three main ways that heat can be transferred: **radiation**, **conduction**, and **convection**.

Imagine yourself playing outside on a hot day. Standing in the sunlight has made you very hot, and you search for some shade. You may feel heat coming off the ground. The transfer of the sun's thermal energy through space is radiation. Radiation has heated you and the ground you're standing on.

Until the late nineteenth century, scientists thought that heat was a substance instead of energy!

Powerful Sun

Radiation from the sun bleaches colors over time. It breaks down bonds in the dye molecules so they reflect a different color than they once did. Today, due to radiation, the flags on the moon have turned white.

Don't Forget!

It's important to remember that temperature is not heat. Temperature is simply a measurement of heat. So if it's really hot outside, that just means there's a lot of thermal energy out there!

Now, what happens if you touch the hot ground? Ouch! It'll probably burn your hand. By touching the ground, the heat transfers directly to your skin. When heat is transferred by one object touching another object, it's called conduction. The thermal energy is transferred from the hot object (the ground) to the cooler object (your hand). This causes the particles in your skin to move faster. And this makes your hand hot!

Thermal energy can also transfer through liquids and gases. When this happens, it is called *convection*. Have you ever watched a pot of water boil? The water gets hot. Bubbles form. Then, the bubbles move in a circular pattern from the bottom of the pot to the top of the pot and back down again. Hot water rises to the top, and the cooler water moves to the bottom. The same thing happens in the air as you play outside on a hot day. This is convection at work.

Conduction at Work

Pots and pans are made from metal because metal conducts, or transfers, heat well. Wood or plastic are added to the handle to prevent you from getting burned. They don't conduct heat well.

How Does Convection Work?

When fluids are heated, they expand. When fluids expand, they become lighter and less dense than the air and other fluids around them. This makes them rise. Once they rise far enough away from the heat source, they start to cool. They sink back down again. And the cycle repeats!

Thermal imaging lets people see the transfer of thermal energy between solids, liquids, and gases.

{ Our oceans circulate using convection! }

Electricity in Motion

Today, one of the most useful forms of energy is electricity. Many items that we use each and every day use this form of energy. Think about what you did today. Did you turn on any lights in your home? Did you watch a television show? Did you do your homework on a computer? All these things use electricity. It's a vital part of our lives. It would be hard to live without it!

Electricity is created by moving electrons. Electrons are small particles of matter. They have a negative charge. They move around the center of an atom. They also like to move from one atom to another. But they can only move to an atom with a positive charge. When electrons jump atoms, they create a small electric charge, or a current of electricity.

Electricity can be transferred and controlled by a **circuit**. Electrons move from the negative side to the positive side of a circuit. If you take a close look at a battery, you'll notice a plus sign on one end and a minus sign on the other. If you connect these two ends with a wire, a circuit is formed.

Positively Amazing

Benjamin Franklin conducted many experiments involving electricity. He also invented many of the terms we use when we talk about electricity. He was the first person to use the terms *positive charge* and *negative charge*. And he came up with the word *battery*.

A battery has stored chemical energy. When you place the battery in a circuit, the energy can be used. The chemical energy converts to electric energy. It travels along the circuit. If you connect a lightbulb to the circuit, the electric energy can be converted into light energy. The lightbulb will turn on, and you can now see in the dark! This is how a flashlight works.

Power plants make large amounts of electricity. This electricity travels along wires and cables from a power plant to your house. Sometimes, you can see these power lines. Other times, they are underground. The walls in your home have wires to push the electricity to each room. Now, all you have to do is flip a switch on the wall to turn on a light. Or you can plug a cord into an outlet. It's that easy!

The first power plant was owned by Thomas Edison and opened in New York City in 1882.

Tiny Power Plants

Batteries are like tiny power plants. If the power goes out, you can use batteries to run a flashlight so you're not left in the dark!

Fossil Fuels

Fossil fuels are made from the remains of living things. Over millions of years, pressure and heat change the remains of plants and animals into things such as natural gas, oil, and coal. Power plants burn coal to make electricity.

Explosive Energy

Explosions are giant releases of energy. Imagine a bomb going off. The stored chemical energy is released into the air as kinetic energy. Bang! Kaboom! Kapow! You can hear it. That sound is energy being released. A big bright ball of fire fills the sky! You can see it. Light energy is released. If you're close enough, and hopefully you're not, you can feel the heat. Thermal energy is released. That one bomb contains a lot of energy that is released in many different forms.

No matter where you look or what you do, energy is involved. You use energy transferred from food to turn the pages in this book. This book itself even contains potential energy. Energy is all around. It's everywhere. Now, the question is, what are you going to do with all that energy?

Reduce Standby Power

Many electronics continue to draw on electricity, even when turned off. This is known as *standby power*. You can reduce this usage and save money by plugging electronics into power strips that can be turned off when not in use.

Nuclear Energy

The United States produces more nuclear-generated electricity than any other country—nearly one-third of the world's total. The second largest producer is France, which generates more than three-fourths of its electricity in nuclear reactors.

Enough sunlight reaches Earth's surface each minute to meet the world's energy demands for an entire year!

Think Like a Scientist

How does solar energy work? Experiment and find out!

What to Get

- 2 latex balloons
- 2 plastic 2-liter bottles
- paint brush
- paint (black and white)

White   Black

What to Do

1 Peel the labels off the bottles and remove the bottle caps.

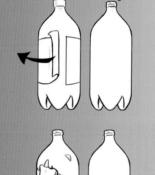

2 Paint one bottle solid black. Paint the other bottle solid white.

3 Place one balloon over the opening of each bottle.

4 Place both bottles in direct sunlight. What changes do you observe? What do you think caused this?

Glossary

chemical energy—energy stored in food, fuel, and other matter

circuit—the complete path that an electric current travels along

conduction—the movement of heat or electricity through something

convection—the movement in a gas or liquid in which the warmer parts move up and the colder parts move down

electric energy—energy made up of a stream of electrons

energy—power that can be used to do something

kinetic energy—energy possessed by an object due to its motion

particles—very small pieces of a large object

potential energy—the energy possessed by an object due to its position; stored energy

radiation—transfer of heat through empty space by waves

sound wave—a wave that is formed when a sound is made and that moves through the air and carries the sound to your ear

work—the transfer of energy that results from a force moving an object

Index

Your Turn!

Economical Energy

Energy costs money. Observe the many ways you use energy in your home. Think about the different ways you can save energy and thereby save some money! Make a poster showing your energy-saving tips. Put the poster up in your home to inspire your family to save some energy (and money)!